Swadl
and c
on old pictu... ,

Mark Bown

1. Swadlincote railway station, on a loop branch line of the Midland's route from Ashby to Burton, where seven passenger trains called daily in each direction (but none on Sundays) in 1910. It closed to regular passenger trains in October 1947 but excursions were run until complete closure of the station in March 1964. This photographic view dates from about 1908.

ISBN 0 946245 81 9

**Printed by
Adlard Print and Typesetting Services,
Ruddington, Notts.**

£2.95

INTRODUCTION

The purpose of this book is to portray Swadlincote, Newhall, Gresley and area through the medium of picture postcards, which were at the height of their popularity in Edwardian times – both as items on which to send messages and as pictures to collect.

Picture Postcards were first published in Britain in 1894, but it was not until a decade later that they began to take off, when in 1902 the Post Office allowed a message to be written on the address side. This meant that the whole of the one side was available for the picture, which obviously gave more scope to the publishers.

Photographic viewcards became very popular and the postcard became the most important way of communicating news or messages in much the same way as the telephone is used today. The years up to 1914 were the `Golden Age' of picture postcards, when millions of cards portraying every imaginable subject were published by a host of national and local firms. Hardly a village or hamlet was not documented at that time by a postcard publisher, though sometimes the number of cards available was unrelated to the size of a community.

The majority of cards illustrated were published by local firms, which was only to be expected. Prominent among these were Siddals of Newhall, F.W. Scarratt of Derby, J.S. Simnett of Burton, and R.B. Hall of Swadlincote. These photographers set out to record life as it was, and the postcards they produced have left us a marvellous record of fashion, leisure and work activities, shops and markets. Publishers are mentioned in the text where the origin of the card is known.

Many of the postcards featured have never before been seen in print, and I hope the book will give many people a chance to re-live a few memories of times and scenes that no longer exist, as well as showing younger people what the area was like earlier this century.

Mark Bown
October 1993

If any readers have postcards, photographs, or other information which might be useful for future publications, please contact me at 30 Victoria Road, Ibstock (0530-262360).

I should like to thank my wife Liesl for assistance with the preparation of this book.

Front cover: a superb picture postcard of Swadlincote High Street around the time of the First World War shows Neales' Tea Stores (grocers), J.J. Needham (clothiers), Theaker's Remnant Stores and Goodhead's bread and confectionery shop. Two horses and carts stand outside the "Stanhope Arms" public house, and the shop on the right is Hunter's Supply Stores. The tracks for the Burton-Ashby Light Railway run down the cobbled street. Card published by Siddals of Newhall in their 'Dorette' series.

Back cover (top): High Street, Swadlincote, seen about 1918 on a postcard by R.B. Hall. Salt Brothers shops were a household name in the town until closure in the early 1980s. The drapery and shoe departments can be seen on this card. On the left is H.B. Dinnis, jewellers, which is still a family concern today.

(bottom): A card by Siddals showing Regent Street, Church Gresley, posted there in September 1911.

Two of the illustrations in this book feature villages in Leicestershire.

2. The Free Library stood on the corner of Highfield Street and Alexandra Road, Swadlincote, and consisted of a reference section, lecture hall, committee room and general news room. The building was demolished in the 1960s due to subsidence. This card, by an anonymous publisher, shows the scene just prior to the library's opening in 1908.

HEARTHCOTE ROAD, SWADLINCOTE.

3. Hearthcote Road, Swadlincote, looking towards the town centre, on a card published by Scarratt of Derby for J.F. Rowley, who owned the Post Office in West Street. Card posted from Burton to Leicester in August 1915.

4. West Street, looking towards Hearthcote Road. In this pre-1914 scene, Alfred George Hall's grocers shop is seen on the left – today it's a do-it-yourself store. Card published by R.B. Hall of Swadlincote.

5. Glebe Street, Swadlincote, taken from Wilmot Road, and featuring an attractive animated scene as children line up for the photographer. The general stores on the corner was last owned by Mrs. Sharp of Lansdown Road and closed in 1983. Another R.B. Hall postcard, published about 1915, but not postally used until some six years later.

6. A small boy can be seen standing outside Wilmot Road Baptist Chapel on this card by Siddals, which was posted at Church Gresley in October 1911. The first stone for the chapel was laid in 1903, but the building is no longer used for religious purposes.

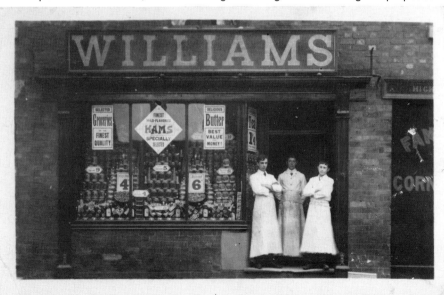

7. Walter J. Williams, grocers, were at 141 Coppiceside, Swadlincote. The staff are pictured in the doorway with a fine display of products for sale. To the left of the shop is the "Barley Mow" pub. This card was sent from the shop and posted in the town on 17th August 1905.

8. The Swadlincote parade (year unknown, but early this century) passes Victoria Row in Coppiceside, the photo being taken from the "Barley Mow" pub. Parades were very popular, both with firms and local people, who found in them some light relief from everyday working life.

CHURCH STREET, SWADLINCOTE.

9. Postcard by Scarratt showing Church Street. Vicarage Road goes off to the right, and just beyond that is the Emmanuel Parish Church. The steeple was demolished in the First World War, becoming unsafe after a zeppelin air-raid. The town's by-pass and a traffic island dominate this scene today.

10. This view of Midway Road is virtually unchanged today. The card, posted at Swadlincote in August 1918, shows a peaceful scene with a delivery cart just to the left of the children. Many of the views in this book feature children standing in the middle of the road, a ploy used by many photographers to enliven their scenes – but something which would be quite dangerous today!

11. Eureka Park, Swadlincote, as it was in the 1930s. The paddling pool has now been filled in and turned into a rose garden. Card by Valentine of Dundee.

12. Belmont Primary School at Swadlincote has changed little since this 1905 view, though the spires have been removed and trees have grown up around the buildings. Church Street is to the left and Belmont Street to the right.

13. Burton-on-Trent Co-operative Societies branch no.9 was in West Street, Swadlincote, and was divided into four departments: (from left to right) tailoring and clothing; general and fancy drapery; boots; and butchery. Just past the Co-op (which closed in the 1980s) is the Wesleyan Methodist Chapel. The card, published by J.F. Rowley of Swadlincote, dates from around 1918, but was not postally used until August 1926.

14. West Street in the 1930s, looking from the town centre, and showing on the left the "Bear Inn" and "Empire Theatre" (the latter was knocked down and replaced by the new "Empire". To the right is Foster's cycle shop, The Post Office, J.W. Belfield's furniture store, the Wesleyan Methodist Chapel, and the Co-op.

15. The "Nag's Head Inn" in High Street, seen here decorated for the Silver Jubilee of King George and Queen Mary in 1935. To the left is Lloyds Bank, while on the right is the *Burton Daily Mail* office and the "Prince of Wales" public house.

16. *"Just a P.C. to show you what Swadlincote is like",* wrote Mary to Miss E. Colby of Wisbech on this card, posted at Burton in July 1927. The view of the Market Place includes a Midland bus stationary outside the Market Hall, which was erected by public subscription in 1861. Bould Brothers' (removal contractors) van is parked outside the "Granville Arms" Foster Brothers (clothiers) and Theaker's (drapers) premises are to the right.

17. Market Place, Swadlincote, showing a typical busy scene as it used to be in front of the Market Hall until the 1960s. A tram heads down Midland Road, followed by Goodhead's bread and confectionery van. The Market Hall clock, with the inscription *"Time the avenger"* reads 6.05 in the evening. Card published by R.B. Hall, and posted at Swadlincote in July 1910.

18. The fire station at Swadlincote originally stood on the site of Green Bank Leisure Centre. This view is taken from Hearthcote Road, with Darklands Road running past the station. Card sent from Swadlincote in May 1905.

19. Swadlincote's horse-drawn fire brigade pose for a photograph outside the station in Darklands Road. The fire engine originated from 1893 and the horses were kept in fields opposite the station. This card was published about 1905.

20. Midland Road, Swadlincote, with Charlie Hextall's fish and game stall on the left, with his cart parked outside. To the right are Foster Brothers, the "Market Inn", and

Austin and Sons ironmongers – the latter were established in the town in 1864. Ault and Tunnicliffe's pottery is in the distance on this c.1930 postcard.

21. A busy scene in Swadlincote High Street, showing two buses of the Birmingham and Midland Omnibus Company. Up until 1927, local transport had been operated by the trams of the Burton-Ashby Light Railways, but due to increasing pressure from the bus companies, the tramway finally closed on 19th February of that year. Postcard published by the Philco Publishing Co. of London for J.W. Belfield of Swadlincote.

22. Woodlands Road, Stanton, was formerly called Council Road. This scene was taken near the "Gate Inn", looking towards Castle Gresley. Most of the cottages to the right have made way for factory premises. Postcard by Siddals, published about 1912.

LOWER MIDWAY, NEAR BURTON-ON-TRENT.

23. A visit to Burton Road, Midway, today would reveal a constant stream of traffic, but the only non-pedestrian on this postcard by Scarratt is a cyclist in the far distance. The cottages to the left were demolished to make way for the "Mason's Arms" public house and car park. Card posted at Midway in September 1913.

24. Siddals took this superb photograph of children in Oversetts Road, Newhall, about 1912. The "Crown" Inn is just to the left of this scene, while the building marked with a cross in the picture is the "Spread Eagle" Inn, which has now been turned into flats. The white building opposite was the "Oversetts" Inn.

25. A view of High Street, Newhall, of c.1910 vintage, looking towards the old Post Office. Newhall Pharmacy now stands on the site to the left, with some of these buildings having been demolished to make more room for the turning into Orchard Street.

26. Another Siddals postcard, showing Main Street, Newhall, looking towards High Street about 1912. The Ebenezer Chapel, built in 1887, is a prominent feature today. Beyond is the "Chesterfield Arms".

27. A view of High Street, Newhall, with three public houses next to each other. From left to right are the "Stanhope Arms", "Angel Inn", and "Holly Bush Inn". The card, published by Siddals, dates from pre-1906, before the lines of the Burton-Ashby tramway were constructed.

28. This card of Bretby Road, Newhall, features the "Thorntree Inn" on the right. The whole scene has shown little change – apart from traffic – in ninety years. Another postcard by local publisher Siddals.

HIGH STREET, SWADLINCOTE.

29. High Street, Swadlincote, as it looked just befo
Mycroft's tobacconists, Woolworth's (before the seco
general goods) and Walter Jones' music shop – with a
pub is on the right, along with Salts Brothers furni
Valentine's and posted at Swadlincote in October 193

outbreak of the Second World War. To the left are
y was added), Wilton & Dytham's bazaar (which sold
'His Masters Voice' banner outside. The "Bull's Head"
hardware department. The card was published by

30. Newhall Post Office on a Siddals card, posted at Swadlincote in September 1913. High Street is off to the right, and the shop with the pole was Hatton's hairdressers.

31. A card of Newhall St. John's Church Band about 1906.

32. Newhall Council School, built in 1894, stood at the junction of Bretby Road and Sunnyside. It was demolished in 1958 due to mining subsidence, and the William Allitt school is now on the site. The card was published for P. Wilton of Newhall Post Office and posted in July 1932.

33. High Street, Woodville, in 1904, looking towards Ashby, and showing W.H. Buckley's "Homelight" tanker passing the chimney and works of the Reliance Pottery. Just past the three-storey houses (now demolished) was the "Prince of Wales" pub, which stood back off the road. The buildings to the right remain today.

34. Around the turn of the century, horses and carts were the main mode of transport until the arrival of the Burton-Ashby Light Railway in 1906. This 1904 card shows High Street, Woodville, looking towards Toll Gate. The buildings featured remain today,

though a garage now stands on the site of Reliance Pottery, behind the wall to the left. On the right can be seen The India & China Tea Company's grocers store, and T.W. Bird's Woodville Clothing Hall, known locally as London House.

35. Swadlincote Road, Woodville, in 1904, with a poster on the hut advertising a "festival of flowers" fair at Swadlincote Town Hall on 20th September. Bloor's crate shop, which made wicker baskets for the transport of local pottery and sanitary ware, is to the left. Sticks can be seen drying outside. Beyond is Bretby Art Pottery.

36. Moira Road, Woodville, on a c.1930 postcard published by Raphael Tuck & Sons of London.

HIGH STREET. WOODVILLE.

37. An early 1930s view of Woodville High Street, taken before the traffic island was installed at the Toll Gate. The Co-op, which closed in January 1984, is on the left and the "New Inn" to the right. Card published by Lilywhite Ltd. and posted from Woodville in October 1933.

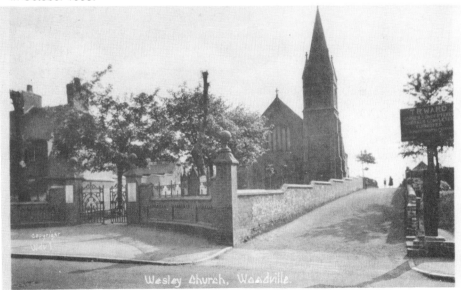

Wesley Church, Woodville.

38. The Wesleyan Church on High Street, Woodville, was built in 1893, but knocked down in the mid-1960s due to lack of use and maintenance costs. A new Methodist Church now stands on this site, and the cottages to the left have been replaced by flats. Tuck postcard from the early 1930s.

39. The Royal Chip Potatoe Dining Car was built for Walter Tootell by Orton & Spooner of Burton. Tootell's had premises in Woodville High Street and at no.5 Market Street, Swadlincote. This superb horse-drawn vehicle was made solely for street sales, and carried the slogan *"Tootell's Fish and Chips feed the brain."* The postcard is of c.1906 vintage.

40. The building on the right on this view of Hartshorne was originally a corn mill, but later used for the manufacture of screws. Water from the pond was used to power the large wheel. The pond has now been filled in and the mill restored and turned into a pub and restaurant, while the chapel in the distance is now a private house. Card published by Siddals, posted at Woodville in October 1910.

41. The "Admiral Rodney", later renamed the "Rodney Inn" on Main Street, Hartshorne, is still a public house, though the "New Inn" has been demolished, and is now the site of the Rodney car park. Card published by R.B. Hall and posted at Woodville in August 1914.

42. High Street, Linton, on a postcard published by Siddals about 1910. Hasbury's shoe shop stood on the left, beside the thatched cottage. Greenfield Drive now leads off to the right of this photo.

43. A quiet country scene at Blackfordby is portrayed on this R.B. Hall card, posted at Coalville in August 1917. The cottages on the right are no longer there, but St. Margaret's school, built in 1889, and the church are still prominent landmarks today.

R.B.Hall Swadlincote.

44. All the local children appear to have turned out for the cameraman in this 1908 scene at Occupation Road, Albert Village. Surprisingly little has changed, though some properties on the right have made way for the entrance into Covert Place.

Opening Day, The Maurice Lea Park, Church Gresley.

45. The Maurice Lea Memorial Park, Church Gresley, was opened in 1929 on common land which had been used as a tip and had become an eyesore. In the picture, a local band marches up Market Street in a parade to celebrate the opening day activities.

46. The cost of enclosing and laying the park was financed by a local man, Herbert Lea, as a memorial to his son, Lieutenant Maurice Bertram Lea, who was killed during the advance on Guillemont on August 18th 1916. The opening day created great interest: this scene looks more like a seaside beach than Gresley Park.

47. This early 1930s view was taken before the pond and fountain were built as a memento of the life and reign of King George V. Bowls was and still is one of the main recreations in the park. The pavilion has recently been replaced by a modern building.

48. The paddling pool was a popular play area with local children, until cleaning costs and doubts about the water purity left it to stagnate and it was eventually filled in. Behind can be seen New England works and many chimneys, common in industrial South Derbyshire but now long since gone. The card was published by R.B. Richards of York.

GROWN FY T. ROBEY.   CHURCH GRESLEY.

49. Thomas Robey shows off his display of cow cabbages, grown as samples to show to local farmers. The left one weighed in at 89lbs, the right at 91lbs. This photo was taken at Robey's grocers shop in New Street, Church Gresley, which closed in the mid-1980s. The family-run wholesale and retail business also had a stall on Swadlincote market.

50. This card of Regent Street, Church Gresley, was posted from the village in September 1905. A milk float delivers to local residents, while children in front of J.T. Evans' grocers and bakers shop seem fascinated by the presence of the cameraman.

Church Gresley Cemetery Gates

51. This impressive building marked the entrance to Church Gresley cemetery on York Road. The building is long gone though the cemetery is still there. Card published by R.B. Hall of Swadlincote, whose printing business was established in 1893, and is still based at Alexandra Road.

52. Gresley Old Hall was built around 1556 out of the materials of the old Gresley Priory. This 1905 view posted from the village shows the Hall when it was divided into cottages, with cow sheds to the right. The building has changed hands several times, and after standing derelict for some time, it later became, and still is, the miners' welfare club. Photographic card, posted from Church Gresley in September 1905.

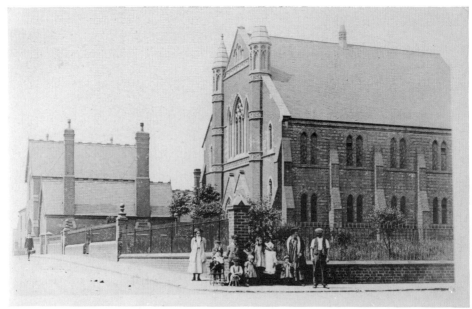

53. The Wesleyan Church, built in 1881, stood opposite York Road School in Church Gresley. It was demolished in the late 1960s due to subsidence, and a new one built in its place. The building to the left marks the entrance to the cemetery. The card was published by Siddals and postally used from Church Gresley in May 1913.

54. Colliers' butchers on Market Street, Church Gresley, displaying a fine selection of meats for sale on a c.1905 postcard. Although the shop pictured is now a private house, the front remains much the same today.

55. The Burton-on-Trent Co-operative Society opened its first shop in the area in 1890. No.14 branch, seen here on this 1910 postcard, was in Church Street, Church Gresley. The grocery department is on the left, while centre was the hardware and right the butchery department. The premises are now used as a video shop.

56. Mount Pleasant Road, Castle Gresley. All the buildings to the left, including the "Railway Inn", have now made way for the "Crown Inn" car park. This pub can be seen further up the road, along with the Primitive Methodist Church.

57. A small boy manoeuvres his horse and trap up Station Road, Castle Gresley, in pre-First World War days. Castle Road runs along the bottom, with the "Drum and Monkey" pub on the right-hand corner. Station Road Methodist Church, the first stones for which were laid in 1904, is on the left. Postcard by Siddals, used in October 1911.